Conjugating Love

By Lois Sullivan

Editor: Dennis Sullivan

Artist: Lois Sullivan

ISBN: 979-8-9999154-0-5

Published by DWS Press

First edition

For permissions or inquiries, contact: DWSpress127@gmail.com

Conjugating Love is a meditative journey through the seasons of the heart, where language and longing intertwine. Lois Sullivan's poetry invites readers to explore love not as a static emotion, but as a verb—conjugated across time, memory, and spiritual reflection. Each poem is a quiet revelation, shaped by the rhythms of nature and the soul's search for connection.

The accompanying watercolor illustrations echo this emotional cadence with tender washes of color and subtle movement. They do not merely decorate the text—they breathe with it, offering visual pauses that mirror the book's contemplative tone. From soft desert hues to ethereal skies, the art evokes both the fragility and resilience of love.

Sullivan's verses move between personal recollection and universal insight, drawing on spiritual themes without dogma. Her language is spare yet resonant, often leaning into silence as much as sound. The poems invite rereading, each time revealing new layers of meaning—like light shifting across a canvas.

This is not a book to be rushed. It is a keepsake for quiet mornings, for moments of reflection, for those seeking beauty in simplicity. Whether read aloud or held close, *Conjugating Love* offers a space for grace and remembrance.

This volume is a tribute to legacy and care—crafted with precision, printed with elegance, and designed to endure. It belongs on shelves where poetry meets spirit, and where art is allowed to whisper.

Artist's Statement

These 62 watercolors by Lois Sullivan are not illustrations—they are meditations.

Painted across decades, they reflect a life steeped in nature, spirit, and memory. From desert blooms and coastal sunsets to symbolic altars and dreamlike figures, each image invites the reader into a moment of reflection.

The paintings appear throughout the book without sequence, echoing the emotional rhythm of the poetry they accompany.

Foreward

Lois envisioned this as her masterwork,
a legacy woven from the depths
of her heart and mind.
Yet time, as it always does, moved forward,
and the rhythms of everyday life intervened.

Now, at last, it is published,
a tribute to her remarkable journey,
a reflection of the life she lived,
the wisdom she shared,
and the love she left behind.

Conjugating Love

THE WAY OF LOVE

"If I speak in human and angelic tongues but do not have love, I am a resounding gong or a clashing cymbal. And if I have the gift of prophecy and comprehend all mysteries and all knowledge; if I have all faith so as to move mountains, but do not have love, I am nothing. If I give away everything I own, and if I hand my body over so that I may boast but do not have love, I gain nothing.

Love is patient, love is kind. It is not jealous, is not pompous, it is not inflated, it is not rude, it does not seek its own interests, it is not quick-tempered, it does not brood over injury, it does not rejoice over wrongdoing but rejoices with the truth. It bears all things, believes all things, hopes all things, endures all things.

Love never fails. If there are prophecies, they will be brought to nothing; if tongues, they will cease; if knowledge it will be brought to nothing. For we know partially and we prophesy partially, but when the perfect comes, the partial will pass away. When I was a child, I used to talk as a child; when I became mature, I put away childish things. At present we see indistinctly, as in a mirror, but then face to face. At present I know partially; then I shall know fully, as I am fully known.

So faith, hope, love remain, these three; but the greatest of these is love."

1 Corinthians, 1

PROLOGUE

Learning to love is like learning to conjugate the verb *To Be*, an unfolding of self and others in the grand tapestry of existence.

Singular	**Plural**
I am	We are
You are	You are
He/She is	They are

I AM

The foundation of love begins with *I am*. It is the first breath of awareness, the quiet recognition of selfhood. As I have been cradled in love—first as an infant, then as a child, and later as an adolescent—so too shall I love as an adult.

I am a reflection of divinity, a soul sculpted in the image of Love itself. With love comes free will, the sacred gift that allows me to shape my destiny. In the stillness of my being, I contemplate, I pray, I choose. I am both the architect and the creation, responsible for the person I become.

YOU ARE

You are the mirror in which I see myself. You are my mother, my father, my first teacher in the language of love. In your eyes, I glimpse my worth. In your voice, I hear the melody of care. Through your tenderness, I begin to understand that I exist—not merely as a body, but as a being worthy of love.

HE/SHE IS

She and He are my companions in discovery, my siblings, my friends. Through them, I awaken to the truth that others, too, carry desires, joys, and sorrows. They laugh, they cry, they hunger, they dream. Their pain is real, their longing familiar. In their reflection, I see the universality of human experience. We are bound by the same needs, the same vulnerabilities, the same capacity for love.

WE ARE

We are the collective, the symphony of individual voices harmonizing into something greater. Love is not merely a solitary act—it is commitment, loyalty, and the daily labor of building something enduring. A marriage, a community, a society—each thrives when we recognize that *we* is the plural of *I*.

YOU ARE

You are the others beyond my immediate circle—the strangers, the distant voices, the unseen lives. To love is to acknowledge their worth, their struggles, their dignity. It is to recognize that every child deserves nourishment, education, and care. It is to dismantle barriers, to replace neglect with compassion, to build a world where no one is forgotten.

THEY ARE

They are the future, the generations yet to come. To love is to think beyond the present, to shape a world where peace is not an ideal but a reality. Wars extinguish life; violence corrodes the soul. We must abandon the sword, as wisdom has long urged us, and embrace the art of dialogue, negotiation, and understanding.

BEING

To be is to exist, but existence alone is not enough. A human being is not merely flesh and bone but a vessel of thought, creativity, and purpose. To be fully alive is to nurture, to protect, to learn, to grow. It is to bring order from chaos, to use our gifts—intellectual, emotional, spiritual—to cultivate harmony.

WELL-BEING

What does it mean to truly *be well*? It is not wealth or status but the quiet fulfillment of life's essentials:

- To have enough to eat.
- To be surrounded by love.
- To dwell in a place of comfort and peace.
- To engage in work that brings joy.
- To receive care for the body, mind, and soul.
- To learn, to grow, to expand the horizons of thought.
- To move, to breathe, to keep the body strong.
- To reflect, to dream, to imagine.
- To play, to laugh, to embrace the lightness of being.
- To give thanks, to rejoice in existence.
- To share abundance with those in need.

To love is to *be*, and to *be* is to love. In this sacred conjugation, we find the essence of life itself.

I AM

I am because love willed me into existence. Love is the seed from which my being has grown, the force that shaped me, the breath that sustains me.

I am unique—an unrepeatable constellation of genes, thoughts, and experiences. No one before me, no one now, and no one after me will ever possess my exact composition. My fingerprints, my voice, my talents, my essence—all singular, all mine.

I am free. Within me lies the power to shape my destiny, to sculpt the soul I wish to inhabit. I am responsible for who I become, for the choices I make, for the effort I invest in refining my gifts. No one else can walk this path for me.

I am a thinking being, capable of wisdom, discernment, and vision. I choose my goals, I determine my course, I bear the weight of my decisions. I am the architect of my own becoming.

I am a descendant of love, and love is my inheritance. It is the legacy I carry, the force that must govern my life.

I am in a perpetual state of growth. From the moment of my conception to the final breath I take, I am evolving.

Each day, each hour, each experience is a lesson, a step toward deeper understanding.

I am flawed. I am sometimes lazy, sometimes impatient, sometimes too intense. But I am also capable of change. My faults are not fixed; they are challenges to overcome, lessons to learn. I am responsible for my own transformation.

I am entrusted with my body, the vessel of my soul. Like a prized racehorse, it requires care, nourishment, and respect. I tend to it with wisdom, seeking healing when it falters, strengthening it when it weakens. My body is not separate from my essence—it is the instrument through which I experience life.

I am a person with faults, but I refuse to let them define me. I will not be enslaved by my weaknesses. I will confront them, challenge them, and rise above them.

FEELINGS

Feelings are the language of the soul. They manifest in many forms:

- **Physical:** I feel warmth, I feel cold, I feel pain, I feel vitality.
- **Intellectual:** I sense truth, I recognize wisdom, I intuit the right path.
- **Emotional:** I feel joy, I feel sorrow, I feel pride, I feel shame.
- **Artistic:** I am moved by music, by poetry, by the grandeur of creation.

Feelings can uplift or imprison. They can inspire growth or breed self-pity. To feel deeply is to be alive, but to be ruled by emotion is to surrender control. When my emotions overwhelm me, I seek guidance. I am not afraid to ask for help.

FEAR

Fear is the shadow that stifles growth, the force that paralyzes the soul. It can make me shrink, hide, deceive, retreat.

I fear love. Why? Because love demands vulnerability. It asks me to risk rejection, to expose my heart, to trust in something greater than myself.

Am I afraid of being hurt? Am I afraid of being seen? Am I afraid of failing? Am I afraid of being unworthy?

Fear is a prison, but I refuse to be its captive.

ENSLAVERS

I am not a slave. I will not surrender my freedom to addiction, to destructive habits, to the chains of complacency.

If I find myself bound—by substances, by toxic relationships, by self-imposed limitations—I will seek liberation. I will fight for my autonomy.

Bad habits are silent enslavers. They creep into my life unnoticed, eroding my discipline, dulling my potential. But I am in charge. I will not allow them to dictate my existence.

RESPONSIBILITY

I am responsible for my life. I will not blame others for my misfortunes. Blame is stagnation; responsibility is growth.

I will seek truth, not convenience. I will embrace wisdom, not ignorance. I will evolve, not remain stagnant.

When I take responsibility, the world opens before me—vast, limitless, full of possibility.

EMPOWERMENT

I am empowered by knowledge, by skill, by discipline.

- I am empowered when I refine my talents.
- I am empowered when I master language, when I wield words with precision.
- I am empowered when I learn to communicate, to listen, to understand.
- I am empowered when I embrace music, numbers, literature, history.
- I am empowered when I expand my mind beyond the boundaries of my own experience.

FAITH, HOPE, AND THE LONG-DISTANCE RUNNER

When one thinks of the process of an education, the years involved, it helps to think of oneself as a long distance runner. It requires faith in one's ability to do it, hope that by perseverance one can accomplish this goal, and love for oneself that it is worth the effort.

LWS 7-15-92

MY BODY

My body is a masterpiece—a living, breathing symphony of complexity and grace. It is more precious than any instrument, more intricate than any machine.

It is my home, my sanctuary, my means of experiencing the world.

I honor it. I nourish it. I strengthen it.

I am vulnerable to pain, to loss, to cruelty. But I am also capable of joy, of ecstasy, of profound connection.

My intellect is the beacon that guides me, the force that allows me to learn, to create, to refine my understanding.

I am a being in motion, in transformation, in pursuit of wisdom.

I am.

TALENTS: The Art of Becoming

To cultivate my talents, I must first grant myself permission to grow. The greatest obstacle to my own success is often myself—the hesitation, the doubt, the fear of failure. But if I am the detour, I am also the path. If I am the cause, I can be the cure.

I ask myself:

- Am I worthy of this pursuit?
- Do I love myself enough to invest in my own potential?
- Am I willing to endure the labor required for the reward of self-fulfillment?
- How do I carve out the time?
- What of my discipline—do I nurture it or neglect it?
- Do I possess the courage to step forward?
- What are the first steps toward mastery?

Creativity is the ability to weave connections, to see patterns where others see fragments. Originality is not invention—it is the unique lens through which I perceive the world, the distinct way I listen, touch, taste, and interpret the symphony of existence.

MY SECRET GARDEN: A Sanctuary of Growth

The life I have built—my marriage, my children, my community—is my secret garden. It is a place of cultivation, where love is planted, nurtured, and harvested.

It has been said that to see life through a single vision is to peer through a knothole—narrow, constrained, incomplete. But in the shared visions of my family, my consciousness expands beyond what I once imagined. Life becomes an adventure, a celebration, a triumph over fear.

As my children grow, they create gardens of their own. Each garden is distinct, yet connected. We walk through one another's landscapes, inhaling the fragrance of new ideas, admiring the colors of different perspectives. And then, enriched, we return to our own spaces, carrying the wisdom of shared experience.

RESPONSIBILITY: The Gateway to Freedom

I am responsible for my life. I will not cast blame upon my parents, my circumstances, or the world for my misfortunes. To blame is to stagnate, to surrender my power to external forces. Growth demands ownership.

I will seek truth—not convenience. I will pursue wisdom—not comfort. I will embrace responsibility—not excuses.

When I take responsibility, the horizon widens. Possibilities unfold where limitations once stood. In accepting the weight of my choices, I grow in grace, in understanding, in the quiet strength of self-awareness.

Responsibility is not a burden—it is the key to becoming.

YOU ARE: The Sacred Bonds of Life

MY PARENTS

You are my beginning. Before I was, you were. Out of your love, I came into being.

You are my cradle, my shield, my fortress. In the security of your arms, I find comfort, warmth, and the quiet assurance that I belong.

You are my nourishment—feeding my body so that I may grow strong, nurturing my heart so that I may believe in my own worth.

You are my first teachers. From you, I absorb the rhythms of life, the unspoken lessons of love and care. I learn from your actions whether I am cherished, whether I am worth the time and effort it takes to be seen, heard, and understood.

You are my first glimpse of God— Whether He delights in me, Whether He loves me, Whether my life has meaning, Whether He will comfort me, Whether He will forgive me when I falter.

You are man and woman, the source of my existence. Yet you are also individuals, with needs of your own:

- You need time to work, to create, to build.
- You need time to learn, to grow, to dream.
- You need time to play, to celebrate, to rest.
- You need time for friendship, for laughter, for renewal.
- You need time for God, for reflection, for the quiet spaces of the soul.
- You need time away from me—to see the world beyond, to return with fresh perspective.
- You need to be refreshed by love, so that you may teach me how to love in return.

MY CHILD

You are my child, born from the love I share with my mate. When I hold you in my arms, I am filled with wonder. You are a complete, intricate being, and I am in awe that life has flowed through me to bring you into existence.

You are my child, and I pledge to love you all the days of my life. I will nourish every part of you—your body, your mind, your spirit.

You are vulnerable, impressionable, and infinitely precious. I will guard the essence of you, treasuring the soul that is uniquely yours.

You are gifted, endowed with talents and aptitudes that will shape the world in ways yet unseen. You carry within you the potential to bring forth new ideas, new perspectives, new solutions.

You are lovable, and I will teach you the ways of love as I know them, so that you may experience the fullness of life.

You are human, and I am human. I will not always be perfect. Love, though pure in intent, sometimes falters in execution. If I fail you, if I fall short, I ask for your forgiveness. May you remember me with compassion.

You are mortal, and I am mortal. One of us may leave this world before you reach maturity. If that day comes, know that you are my treasure, worth everything good and beautiful.

You are my responsibility, yet life may demand that I entrust you to another. If I cannot keep you, if circumstances separate us, know that my love remains unwavering. I think of you every day. I pray that one day you will understand the depth of my sacrifice, the immensity of my love.

You are my child, and I thank God for you.

MY GRANDCHILD

You are my grandchild, and once again, I am filled with wonder.

You are fresh, exquisite life, and I am entranced by your presence, by the purity of your being.

You are the child of my child, the continuation of love, the embodiment of all that has come before. You are the delight of my heart, the gift of my maturity, the whisper of eternity.

You are my grandchild, and through you, I see life anew. You grant me perspective, reminding me of the cycles of existence, the unfolding of generations.

You are my hope for a better world. Your gifts are many, and your contributions will shape the future.

You are the promise of tomorrow, and I cherish you beyond words.

HE/SHE IS: The Tapestry of Human Connection

HE/SHE IS MY SIBLING

My brother, my sister—older or younger—offers me another lens through which to see the world, another rhythm in the symphony of my learning.

My sibling is my first playmate, the architect of my childhood landscape. Together, we build and rebuild, shaping the foundation of our understanding—learning to get along, to compromise, to navigate the delicate balance between self and other.

My sibling is a lesson in sharing, in fairness, in justice. We divide, we give, we take, we learn.

My sibling is a person in their own right, with an equal claim to existence, an equal share of rights and privileges.

My sibling is the child, too, of my mother and father. Together, we are a family—a unit, a team, a constellation of souls bound by love and lineage. We work, we play, we celebrate.

My sibling is a child of God, just as I am. We hold hands in the sacred circle of family, bound by the invisible thread of love.

As we grow, the building blocks of childhood transform into the architecture of maturity. We learn to forgive old wounds, to release past rivalries. We delight in each other's triumphs, take pride in each other's choices, cherish each other's children. We honor each other's homes, respect each other's paths, and find joy in both our similarities and our differences.

When my sibling is ill, we stand together. We pray, we comfort, we uplift. We bring laughter to lighten the weight of suffering, we offer courage in the face of fear. We serve each other with the gift of memory, weaving the past into the present as a balm for the soul.

3

HE/SHE IS MY FRIEND

He/she is my friend—a presence that enriches, a perspective that expands my understanding of life.

Through friendship, I glimpse the diversity of human experience:

- Some parents are more or less affluent than mine.
- Some are more or less courteous, more or less generous, more or less thoughtful.
- Some are divorced, some are single.
- Some are of a different race, a different culture, a different faith.
- Some grew up in distant lands, shaped by traditions unfamiliar to me.
- Some celebrate different holy days, follow different rules, hold different beliefs.

He/she is my childhood friend. Together, we examine life, testing its boundaries, questioning its meaning. We learn to fight and reconcile, to disagree and remain steadfast. We discover the joy of companionship, the art of teamwork, the beauty of shared laughter.

He/she is the friend of my maturity. We listen, we counsel, we celebrate each other's victories. We grieve for each other's losses, stand beside each other in times of need. We honor our differences, cherish our memories, and remain loyal in love and friendship.

HE/SHE IS OTHER

He/she is unique—a life unfolding in ways I may never fully understand.

He/she is worthy of my respect, my courtesy, my recognition. For he, too, is a human being—a child of God, a fellow traveler in the journey of existence.

He/she is shaping their own destiny, whether with intention or by circumstance, navigating the world according to their resources, their experiences, their choices.

He/she is a person who had a mother and a father—who may have been cherished or neglected, taught the goodness of life or left to discover it alone, loved in maturity or abandoned in uncertainty.

He/she is a stranger, yet not unknown. A human being with personhood, vulnerability, needs, desires, weaknesses, illnesses, strengths, potentials, possibilities.

He/she is, like me, a seeker of meaning, a bearer of burdens, a holder of dreams.

WE ARE: The Sacred Bonds of Unity

WE ARE SPOUSES

Scott Peck once said of his wife: *"The purpose and function of Lily is to grow to be the most of which she is capable, not for my benefit but for her own and to the glory of God."*

We are one—bound by love, by commitment, by the sacred promise to honor and serve each other. We are two in one—distinct souls intertwined, two perspectives woven into a single journey. We are one, and in that oneness, love is nurtured, renewed, and strengthened. We are two in one, and our gifts, our talents, our wisdom are doubled. We are one in purpose, yet two in personality, enriching the three dimensions of our existence—mind, body, and spirit. We are one partnership, one family, one shared life. We are two in one in our labor—the work of our hands, our minds, our hearts. We are one in harmony, yet two in creative potential. We are one with two perspectives, two histories, two voices. We are two in one spirit of love.

We are shaped by our pasts— Different mothers, different fathers, different childhoods, different homes, different ancestors, different teachers, different customs, different vulnerabilities, different strengths, different fears, different hopes, different talents, different values.

Yet in our differences, we are enriched.

We are bound by traditions, rituals, and the art of living:

- We listen to each other with full attention.
- We respect each other's opinions.
- We appreciate each other's thoughtfulness.
- We comfort one another in sorrow.
- We honor each other's wisdom—both intuitive and analytical.
- We work together toward shared goals.
- We are loyal, faithful, and steadfast.
- We are keepers of our love.
- We act out our love, not just in words but in deeds.
- We live each day with intention.
- We celebrate life together.
- We grow in love.

Year after year, we add to the liturgy of our love. We are keepers of the flame.

WE ARE FAMILY

We are a family, bound not just by blood but by awareness.

We are aware that each of us has needs of our own. We are aware of each other's need for solitude. We are aware that each of us carries dreams. We are aware that each of us has an inner world, a separate destiny. We are aware that each of us possesses unique gifts, talents, vulnerabilities. We are aware of the importance of celebration, of joy, of shared laughter. We are aware of the comfort found in the embrace of family. We are aware that love requires time, patience, and presence.

When death comes, we stand together. We grieve, we remember, we hold each other in sorrow. Our loved one has passed through the veil into the unknown, yet they remain—etched in the deepest chambers of our hearts.

We are alone once more—just the two of us. The children have grown, moved on, built lives of their own. It is not an *empty nest* but a fullness—a quiet contentment in knowing we have done our best.

We are rich in shared memories, in goals accomplished, in love sustained. We are in the third trimester of life, yet still learning, still growing. We are survivors, and we know the joy of commitment. We are blessed with the aura of love.

Rainer Maria Rilke once wrote: *"Once the realization is accepted that even between the closest human beings infinite distances continue to exist, a wonderful thing side-by-side can grow up, if they succeed in loving the distance between them which makes it possible for each to see the other whole against the sky."*

WE ARE INTERACTING

We are in the process of living, of learning, of growing together.

Sometimes you act in haste; sometimes I react without thought. Sometimes you act with energy; sometimes I respond in exhaustion. Sometimes you act with optimism; sometimes I react with doubt. Sometimes you act generously; sometimes I respond selfishly. Sometimes you act courageously; sometimes I react fearfully. Sometimes you act slowly, with shyness; sometimes I react with bluntness. Sometimes you act under stress; sometimes I respond with understanding.

Ideally, we interact with thoughtfulness, with sensitivity, with compassion. Ideally, we interact with love.

WE ARE STRONG IN UNITY

Let there be light—light in our minds, in our hearts, in our understanding of human dignity.

Let there be no more slums, no more barrios, no more forgotten souls left to believe they are unworthy.

Let us take one family, move them into a home of dignity. Let us teach them, if they do not know, how to care for their space, how to cultivate beauty. Let us teach them, if they do not know, how to manage their resources wisely. Let us teach them, if they do not know, how to nourish their bodies, their children, their spirits. Then, let us take another family, and another, until poverty is no longer a condition but a memory.

We are strong when we unite for the common good. We are strong when our goals align, when our hands work together. We are strong when we pool our strengths, when we lift each other up.

We can be strong in love, yet weak in addiction—alcohol, drugs, gambling, self-destruction. But when we unite, we create order out of chaos. When we stand together, we rise. Unity is the bond that makes us strong.

YOU ARE: The Reflection of Humanity

You are vulnerable. Once I truly comprehend the fragility at the heart of every human being, every family, every race, every culture, every society, I will begin to build a bridge of understanding—a bridge of friendship, of compassion, of unity.

You are constantly expanding my awareness, revising my understanding, challenging my assumptions. You are continually offering me knowledge of a world larger than my own. You are steadily enlarging my frame of reference, urging me to see beyond my own existence. You are courageously asking me to examine my motives—whether they stem from selfishness, greed, or the pursuit of the common good. You are encouraging me to make decisions with greater awareness, greater wisdom, so that my actions do not wound, do not destroy, do not pierce the vulnerability within you. You are making me aware that to love you is to care for your well-being, to recognize your dignity, to honor your humanity.

You are:

- The marginalized, the unseen, the unheard.
- The seekers, the believers, the doubters.

- The oppressed, the resilient, the hopeful.
- The ones who have been cast aside, yet refuse to be forgotten.

You are:

- Black, Hispanic, Indigenous, Asian.
- Atheist, Christian, Jewish, Muslim, Buddhist.
- The "Have-Nots," the Non-Conformists, the Handicapped, the Aliens.
- The Latch-Key Children, the Mentally Ill, the Criminals and the Victims.
- The Street People, the wanderers, the displaced.

You are a person. When we speak unkindly, when we wound with words, when we diminish with cruelty, we do not merely harm you—we diminish ourselves.

If we strip you of your worth, we strip ourselves of our own humanity.

"What I do unto others, I do unto myself."

You are a constellation of stars, a universe of wisdom, a wealth of untold stories. You are worth more than jewels, yet we confine you to slums and barrios. We legislate your wages, yet deny you the education to rise beyond them. We criticize your lack of skills, yet keep your children from our schools.

You are night to our day, humility to our arrogance, witness to our indifference. We have profited from your bondage, turned bitter in the face of your joy. We have sent your young men to war, silenced the flowering of your young women.

You have been Abel, we have been Cain. In shame, let us close the door to that dead end. Let wisdom guide us, hand in hand, So peace and love may heal this land.

Ángel de los Pescadores

THEY ARE:

They are the Mothers for Peace—the guardians of love, the protectors of life.

They want good things for their children—things that nourish the spirit, cultivate joy, and shape them into whole, well-adjusted beings. They want education that does not merely instruct but inspires, so that their children may fulfill their potential. They want nourishment that sustains, that protects against the diseases of excess, imbalance, and insufficiency.

They are the Mothers for Peace who reject the illusion of military buildup, who see through the fallacy of *overkill*. They are the Mothers for Peace who refuse the logic of *an eye for an eye, a tooth for a tooth*. They are the Mothers for Peace who will bring about change—not through force, but through love, through courage, through the unwavering commitment to a better world.

They are the generations who came before us—the architects of our present, the pioneers of our knowledge, the builders of our foundations. They are the generations who will come after us—the inheritors of our choices, the ones who will carry forward the legacy we leave behind.

Do I love them enough to make the world better for them? Do I care enough to fight for clean air, for pure water, for a thriving Earth? Am I willing to sacrifice convenience for sustainability, luxury for preservation? Will I lead, teach, research, legislate, vote—so that the world they inherit is not poisoned by our neglect?

They are the future. And the future is in my hands.

The Cradle Moon

www.ingramcontent.com/pod-product-compliance
Lightning Source LLC
LaVergne TN
LVHW052356100826
845147LV00013B/853

9798999915405